Potty Mastery

A Child-Centered Approach to Toileting

by **Joan Morgenstern**
with Dr. Becky Bailey

For information regarding permissions, write to
Conscious Discipline, LLC., 648 Trestle Point, Sanford FL 32771.

P: 407.366.4293 | ConsciousDiscipline.com

ISBN: 978-1-7373449-9-5

Cover and Page Design: Jennifer Sucart
Editor: Julie Ruffo

About the Authors

 **Joan Morgenstern** is an educator, author, former early childhood director and certified parent coach with 30+ years of experience. She is passionate about helping parents find their footing and gain confidence through her workshops, seminars, classes, and one-on-one coaching sessions. Joan has worked with hundreds of families, helping parents confidently face every stage of a child's development, including the toileting process. *Potty Mastery*'s child-centric approach assists parents in attuning with their child's needs and empowers them to see children as capable. Joan believes this perspective shift plays an essential role in supporting children's potty success.

 **Dr. Becky Bailey** is an award-winning author, educator, and internationally recognized expert in childhood education and developmental psychology with 35+ years of expertise in her field. She is the creator of Conscious Discipline, which has impacted more than 17 million children while inspiring and training more than 3.5 million educators and caregivers. Conscious Discipline facilitates an intentional shift in adults' understanding of behavior via the Conscious Discipline Brain State Model. It then provides specific trauma-responsive, research-backed strategies for responding to each child's needs with wisdom. This highly effective approach has been shown to increase self-regulation, healthy connection, empathy, intrinsic motivation, positive regard and achievement in children and adults.

*To all the pre-potty tots and their adult leaders.
Remember, you've got this! Keep going!*
Joan Morgenstern

To Walker and all of the future generations.
Dr. Becky Bailey

Table of Contents

Potty Mastery Foreword

If you have searched the web or the library for books to help move your child from diapers to toileting, you will find the words "Toilet Training" and "Potty Training." What if children don't need us to train them to use the toilet? What if they need us to be attuned, communicative parents and caregivers who support the learning process of an innate developmental milestone, a milestone that is unique for each child?

When we shift our adult mindset from "getting children to use the toilet" to "helping children be successful at toileting," we are on our way to facilitating Potty Mastery.

In a world full of sticker charts, comparisons and pressures, *Potty Mastery: A Child-Centered Approach to Toileting* is a breath of fresh air that will help you attune with your child's needs and recognize this time for what it is: An expression of autonomy and growth for your child. It's a milestone you may both feel deeply, but it's the child's body so they are ultimately in charge of it.

The beauty of Potty Mastery is the recognition that this is your child's journey. Rather than *training* your child, you will support them in developing a skill. (Do you really want them to "go peepee on the potty for Mommy" or do you want them to go to the bathroom for themselves?) In this book, you will learn to recognize cues that your child is ready to begin the process and learn how to set the stage for success. Then you'll discover how to support them, honor their experiences, handle common hiccups, and encourage them from the heart rather than from the candy dish.

A pottying approach like this has been a long time coming. Joan Morgenstern is a 30-year parent coach and early childhood professional, and a longtime practitioner of Conscious Discipline. When she showed me her manuscript, it was immediately clear that her approach would fill a gap experienced by many families and early childhood personnel who knew traditional potty *training* methods like charts and rewards were missing something. That "something" is the opportunity to attune and connect with the child. When we honor the child's experience— as Potty Mastery does— we create opportunity after opportunity to strengthen our relationship rather than strain it, to encourage resilience rather than increasing anxiety, and to open the door to playful learning instead of inducing stress.

Our ability to see children as capable plays an essential role in their achievement. Potty Mastery cultivates confidence by differentiating between "mastery" and "perfection," and by encouraging adults to shift their focus from the mistakes and messes to the micro-achievements along the way. Shifts like these transform the pottying process for adults and children alike and draw from the core methodologies of Conscious Discipline.

More than 25 years ago, I created Conscious Discipline as a pathway for us to discipline differently than we were disciplined, break the cycle of "do as I say, not as I do," and learn how to discipline ourselves and our children with assertiveness, self-regulation and compassion (rather than permissiveness, aggression and guilt). Now, Conscious Discipline is practiced in millions of homes, childcare centers, schools and districts around the globe. My core parenting book for Conscious Discipline is *Easy to Love, Difficult to Discipline*, and it is unique from other forms of guidance because it:

- Defines discipline not as something you do to children, but something you develop within them.
- Teaches new skills to the adult first and the children second, empowering you to become the mindful parent you want to be.

It has been my honor to contribute to *Potty Mastery: A Child-Centered Approach to Toileting*, and to see it released under the umbrella of Conscious Discipline. Like Conscious Discipline, Potty Mastery seeks a more compassionate, more self-regulated and more attuned way of existing in this world that enhances cooperation, reduces power struggles and strengthens the bonds between us.

Potty Mastery, like Conscious Discipline, teaches us that we are meaning-makers for our children. Children create their earliest beliefs about themselves through the millions of tiny moments they experience in early childhood. Adults influence how children perceive their bodies—possibly for the rest of their lives. Potty Mastery advances a process we hope for all children: the development of love for oneself. I wish you many treasured moments together during this beautiful, messy journey of parenting and potty learning, and I wish you well in all things.

- Dr. Becky Bailey
Creator of Conscious Discipline

Introduction

You're in the bathroom at home. In one hand, a diaper. In the other, a pair of rocket-ship underwear. In front of you, the toilet. On the floor, a scowling toddler. On your face, a baffled expression.

Welcome to the world of the potty.

I'm guessing that as the parent of a young child, you've thought once or twice about potty-*training*. It's supposed to be hard, right? Tears, rage, pants-pooping? Battles of wills in grocery-store restrooms, fits of frustration in the aisles of big-box stores? Sometimes you think your child is probably going to be the one who has to wear diapers until they are fifteen because. You. Just. Cannot. Figure. This. Out.

How in the world are you going to explain to this very cute but very stubborn and very small person that from now on, they are to place their poop and pee in this bucket-like thing instead of in the diaper that has been snuggled up against their bottom every minute of the day since birth?

Breathe deeply. Potty *training* – or potty *mastery*, as I like to call it (more on that later) – can not only be easy but maybe even a little fun! We're going to walk through a brain-compatible, developmentally appropriate and compassionate process for potty mastery step by step, and I'm going to show you it doesn't have to be a tearful, rageful power struggle. Instead, it can be a way for you and your child to do something important together, as a team... perhaps for the first time, but certainly not for the last.

Myth Vs. Fact
See if you can identify the potty myth vs. the potty fact.

1. **Myth or Fact?** Pull-ups are a useful potty mastery tool. Get a box today!

2. **Myth or Fact?** Children should stop wearing diapers (when they are awake) as soon as you start potty mastery.

3. **Myth or Fact?** Daytime and nighttime dryness often occur at different times.

4. **Myth or Fact?** Rewards like toys or candy are great ways to help children through potty mastery.

5. **Myth or Fact?** Parents can control whether or not their child uses the potty.

Answers

1. **Myth: Pull-ups are a useful potty mastery tool.**
   Pull-ups are really just diapers that slide up and down. They're great for practicing dressing and undressing but other than that – save your money. Go straight from diapers to underpants.

2. **Fact: Children should stop wearing their daytime diapers when you start potty mastery.**

   How well can you learn how to swim by standing on the side of the pool? Swimming and potty mastery have one big characteristic in common: they both require getting wet. Children who are starting potty mastery are going to need to learn what it feels like to be wet in underpants; you just can't do that while wearing a diaper! Additionally, children can't interpret ambiguity. To them, diapers are meant to hold pee and poop. Underpants are meant to keep clean and dry.

3. **Fact: Peeing in the daytime and peeing in the nighttime are not necessarily one and the same.**

   They might seem like they're the same: same child, same bladder, same fluid. But in fact, most children learn daytime dryness and nighttime dryness at different times.

4. **Myth: Rewards like toys or candy are great ways to help children through potty mastery.**

   External rewards build external motivation. Children begin to seek success to achieve the prize rather than for the success itself. Honoring your child's accomplishments in an authentic way builds intrinsic motivation and strengthens your relationship in ways no candy, trinket or sticker ever could. The reward for success becomes success itself, not the toy.

5. **Myth: Parents can control whether or not a child uses the potty.**

   Potty mastery is a child's job. Only they can put their pee and poop in the potty. You can't do it for them. Parents are the support system, the cheerleaders and the coaches, but children are in charge.

1

Letting Go

As a parent, you can probably think of approximately 12,837,462 good reasons to begin tackling the potty. Diapers are expensive. They are wasteful. They're harmful to the environment. They're a pain to haul around. They are smelly. And after a while, what happens inside a diaper becomes, shall we say, "adult-sized." The whole experience of changing a fully mobile child's diaper seems significantly less appealing than when that child weighed nine pounds and couldn't lift their own head. Transitioning to the potty just seems *right*. Not to mention that many preschools require children to be potty-trained before they can attend. Besides, let's confess, no one wants to be that parent on the playground with a big galumphing preschooler still in diapers while all the other (perfect) children are frolicking around with petite rear ends clad in cotton.

All of these *are* good reasons to begin using the potty. But they're our reasons; adult reasons. There's someone else involved here (shocker!) and that person doesn't care if a month's worth of diapers costs as much as a candlelit dinner for two. They don't care that their bedroom practically needs professional fumigation after one of those monster diaper changes. For this person, the real reason – the only reason – to learn the potty is that getting out of diapers is one more step toward autonomy and self-care. For your child, potty mastery is just one more accomplishment. It's one more skill of daily living, just like when they learned to use a fork and hold a toothbrush. Going on the potty means one more step towards developing independence and growing up.

I work in a pediatrician's office. I have taught parenting classes for over a decade. I've studied children and their development academically and professionally. I've been a classroom teacher, a parent coach, a school director and a teacher of teachers. And most importantly, I'm a mother of three. My techniques have been researched and road-tested by families in all these arenas as well as by my own kids. Although the individual journeys to potty mastery may look very different, there are overarching principles that are universally helpful for supporting potty success in a way that sustains healthy relationships, mindset, self-concept, and wellbeing.

As we stare together down the long tunnel of potty mastery, let me begin by saying: Your child can do this. You can do this. It's not going to be the most difficult task you've mastered — like learning to parallel park or speaking a second language — and it's not going to be as easy as gazing at the sky on a beautiful day. Potty mastery lies somewhere in between.

There are only two big ideas to remember at the outset.

The first big idea is that potty mastery is part of parenting. It's no different from helping your child to choose healthy food to eat, making sure they're wearing snow boots after a blizzard or comforting them when they bump their head. Many parents tackle potty mastery as if the process is some beast that exists separate from the usual routines, practices and values they hold dear. That approach might work okay if learning to use the potty was a linear, well-defined path that begins with potty boot-camp and ends with a toilet-trained child. But it's not.

Potty mastery is a process that you and your child work through together. It will feed off the energy that you put into it. If you go in combative, tense and negative, then that's exactly how the learning will proceed. If you enter in relaxed, flexible and confident, then your child will feed off that energy as well. You know your child. You know yourself. You've built a beautiful foundation so far as a parent. You've held this child against you, fed them,  changed them and worked their hands through many tiny sleeve-holes. Your knowledge of your own child will guide you through this process.

If your child loves routine, you'll incorporate that into their potty learning. If your child does better with creative flexibility, you'll try that. You're not a rookie. You have a lot of tools in your parental toolbox and I'm here to tell you that those tools are your most valuable assets as you begin potty mastery.

The second big idea to remember is that you are not in control of this process. That can be a scary, startling thought. Somewhere the idea that a parent's job is to control their child's behavior took root in our collective unconscious: A well-mannered child who conforms to the usual standards is a sign of a good parent, while the parents of children who display behaviors outside of the comfortable middle have failed in some way. It's time to shift that paradigm. Parenting is about self-control, not child control. We are responsible for our actions and decisions, and our children are responsible for theirs.

Our responsibilities are to:

- Teach children skills they are missing
- Create the structures that will help to facilitate our children's success
- Provide the opportunity to test and experiment (including the opportunity to fail because failure is a powerful teaching tool)
- Sooth, comfort, and reteach children through their failures
- Celebrate their successes

Our job is not to control them; it's to co-create with them. We can no more make an infant who hates peas swallow a mouthful of mashed peas than we can make a child who is unwilling to sit on the potty do their business. Your child is in the driver's seat, strapped in, helmet on, staring down that long track. You are the pit crew that races up to change the tires and offers the driver encouragement.

Trying to control the potty process for your child will exhaust both you and them. Once you accept that your child has autonomy over their poop and pee, then you can switch to the support role. You're saying to your child, "I understand that this is your job. I'm here to help you and we're going to do it in a way that's comfortable for both of us." Being your child's support, rather than their director, is going to help your child feel strong, confident and empowered.

When we accept that children are in control of their bodies and their behavior, we recognize their success as their own. Our success as a parent is no longer linked to what our child puts in the toilet. That action is theirs to own, an accomplishment that transcends stickers and treats and builds intrinsic motivation. Intrinsic motivation is an inner yearning that leads us to do things for the positive feelings associated with the outcome, instead of those associated with a tangible reward. It becomes about the accomplishment, and not the stuff. Children already possess this internal motivation, but in our rush to have them diaper-free, we often deprive them of it. Instead, we look to gain control of the situation through edicts, rewards and pleas to "Go peepee for Mommy!".

When we put our children in the driver's seat, they'll eventually want to control their poop and pee. They want to feel powerful, accomplished and full of "I did it" energy! Potty mastery teaches them the social behaviors necessary to be successful: where to put it, when to put it there and how to do it. We're not forcing children to do anything when we help them with potty mastery. We're simply providing them with the tools and structures they need to learn a new skill and feel proud of themselves as they do it!

Potty Mastery? What Is That?

As I began writing this book, I started calling potty-*training* "potty mastery." I'm not just being picky or cute. These words really do matter. Using a different label for this process can completely change how both you and your child think about what you're doing.

Let's ponder for a moment the word "training." Dogs are trained. Horses are trained. Unruly hair can be trained. Training implies that by doing something in a certain order, over and over, with rewards and corrections (in the case of the dog and the horse, but not necessarily with the hair), something or someone will change. They'll stop performing an action the old way. They'll start doing it a new way.

I don't know about you, but "training" just doesn't fit in with my parenting philosophy. I don't say that I "trained" my daughter to learn to read. You wouldn't say, "We're so excited! We trained our child to walk last week." "We're really working on bike-training right now." Or, during those preteen years, "He's almost ready for dating training." Even driving is "driver's education" not "driver training." Yet, when it comes to the potty, we're all about the "training" as if it's a one-way, "give stimulus and receive results" process. Instead, with this book, we're trying to think of the potty as one milestone among many you and your child will experience together.

Mastering the potty is no different from learning to read or becoming responsible enough (and old enough) to date. We're just taught that it's different. So, I propose that we throw out the word "training," and all its rigid implications. Instead, as you've already noticed, I've chosen "potty 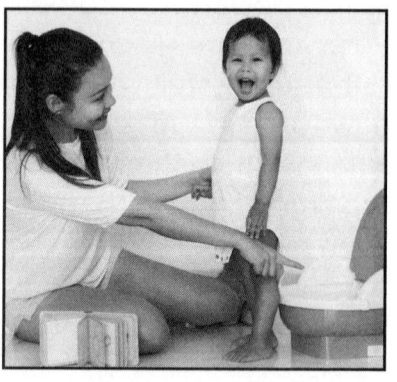 mastery." To master something is to face it, take it on and make it part of your skillset. Potty mastery is not something you have to train your child to do. It's something your child will do *on their own*, with you as support.

A Closer Look at Training Vs. Mastery	
Training	**Mastery**
Something we do to another individual with the goal of achieving a specific outcome	The process of acquiring a new skill that develops over time
Repetition, drills, rewards, punishments	Understanding, interpreting, structuring, adjusting, learning
"You need to do this."	"You'll be learning how to do this."
Making someone do something by the force of your own will	Supporting someone's mastery by offering help and encouragement

Your child is the one who will work toward mastering the potty. No one needs to train them. Instead, they'll need their pit crew to back them up... That's you!

I find it helpful to think about two different methods of potty learning: habit training and spontaneous recognition. Habit-training is the "training" column of the chart above. And spontaneous recognition is the "mastery" column. Habit-training is what we usually think of when the word "potty-*training*" floats around. It's the idea that by repeating a routine over and over, pooping and peeing in the potty will become a learned habit. Habit-training functions on the same basic system that gerbil-training uses: hold a sunflower seed in your hand every time you open the cage, and the gerbil will soon learn that cage-opening equals a treat and will run up to your hand.

In the case of the potty, a child repeats the same motions at the same time every day: after breakfast, they have potty time with a book until poop happens. This isn't a *bad* system. In fact, it's an okay one. After all, even adults like to have quiet time on the toilet at certain times during the day.

The real problem with habit-training is that the adult owns this system. The adult decides when and where and how the child is going to potty. With habit training:

> The adult has to convince the child, "It's time for potty!"
>
>> What happens if the child crosses their arms and says, "No"? (Toddlers are great at this.)
>
> Generally, the adult shifts to bribes: "Come on," the adult wheedles. "You'll get your jellybean."
>
>> Sensing the adult's investment in this potty thing, the child counters, "I don't want a jellybean!"
>
> And we're off to every family's favorite place: Power Struggle Central!

An unfortunate side-effect of this approach is that the whole focus of the conversation has now shifted from using the potty to who is in power. Guess who loses every time?

(You... And your relationship.)

Spontaneous recognition is the opposite of habit training. It is the awareness that lies at the heart of potty mastery. With spontaneous recognition, the child thinks, "Oh! I need to go pee!" They're aware of the sensation in their own bodies, just as you are when you need to pee. They make the decision to go on the potty. They might need a little assistance from you for the logistics, but the whole process – from listening to their body to choosing the potty rather than having an accident – is coming from within. This is the process we are going to focus on throughout this book.

2

Know Your Child

The potty mastery process will be smoother and less stressful if you remember you're not dealing with a generic child. You're dealing with your own child, whom you know better than anyone in the world. I'm not the expert on your child. You're the expert. If you get into this process and your gut is telling you, "This is not working," then listen. You are in charge of adjusting, adding and discarding parts of our plan so that what remains works best for *your* unique child.

Take a minute and think about your child's temperament – how they react to life in general. This will influence how they take on potty mastery. In general, most people (including children) fall into one of the following loose categories: easy temperament, slow-to-warm-up temperament or strong temperament. Children with generally easy temperaments might be more flexible than others. They may readily accept a new learning process, such as potty mastery, without much protest.

Children with slow-to-warm temperaments need to take their time. These children are often "watchers." They'll observe for a long time before they do something. Allowing these children to tackle the potty at their own pace will help them feel safe. Forcing them to do something before they are ready will only reinforce any sense of reluctance they might have, and could impede their future learning, relationships and feelings of self-esteem.

Strong temperament children want to do things *themselves*. Often, this comes from a need to gain power and/or control. That's fine for potty mastery. Let these children have control of the process. Let them exert their power under your leadership. If you get sucked into a back-and-forth power struggle with your strong-willed child over the potty, *you will lose*. Remember, they are in control of their bodies, not you. Instead, involve them in the planning, provide acceptable choices and boundaries to navigate within, and encourage them to maintain control over as much of the process as possible.

Looking for an Easy Solution? Stop Reading Here

This scene might feel familiar: You bump into a friend at Target. She's got her child, you've got yours. Her cart is loaded, *loaded*, with juice, candy, cleaning wipes, spray, a potty and underwear. "We're doing potty boot camp!" she says with both glee and desperation. Maybe you even experience a fleeting pang of envy as you glance at your own happily non-potty-trained child, sitting placidly in the cart like they could happily wear diapers until they're fifty. Your friend seems to have it pretty well together. Maybe you should try... stop. Stop right there. Step away from the potty-boot camp cart and take three deep breaths. I'm going to let you in on a little secret: Potty boot camp does not work. It does not help. Here's a bigger secret, one that will really blow your mind: Rewards and bribes don't work long-term either. I know, crazy, right?

I know, I know: I've just taken *Potty Training's Greatest Hits* list and ripped it to shreds right in front of your face. Before you slap this book closed and throw it in the trash, let me reassure you that there are many, many tools that do work. Recognition and encouragement come to mind. As does routine. Oh, and patience. Patience, above all.

So, this is where you stop me to say, "But potty boot camp worked for so-and-so!" Potty boot camps are so popular that everyone knows someone who did it successfully. They are popular because they're quick and they're prescriptive. It's enticing to think you can buy a cartload of stuff with a diaper-wearing child on a Friday and prance out of the house on Monday morning, proud and free in the land of cotton. Potty boot camps work for a *parent's* schedule. But that schedule may not be the child's schedule. Your child has been pooping and peeing in a diaper for two, two-and-a-half, or three years. Lasting change is going to take longer than forty-eight hours.

For most families, expecting your child to master the potty in a weekend is going to make you impatient if the progress is slower. It puts pressure on an already high-stakes process. Bootcamps place unnecessary stress on you, your child and your relationship. And here's the kicker: families who are successful with potty bootcamp are the ones who would have been successful without the bootcamp. Simply put, those children were already motivated to take the plunge.

"Okay, fine," you may say. "I can see the rationale against potty boot camps. But no *rewards*? How is a sticker or a piece of candy a bad thing?"

Well, they're not a bad thing. They're just not the magic bullet that we often think they are, nor are they the most effective long-term motivators.

As an educator, I also feel strongly that rewards are pride killers. We want our children to feel inherent, true pride in themselves for learning new skills like using the potty. We want that feeling to come from inside themselves, not implanted into them by us, the parents. When we offer an outside reward ("You peed in the potty! Here is your treat"), we're saying "This is my show. I'm offering the satisfaction, which I'm giving to you in the form of a tangible reward. What you feel inside yourself is neither here nor there."

The candy or the sticker is a distraction from the inherent pride and self-worth your child can feel when they use the potty. It pivots the focus to the reward and away from the child's accomplishment. It's an incentive, yes, ("Go pee in the potty and you'll get your jellybean!") but it chips away at the child's ability to look at the potty and think, "I want to use this thing. Let me figure out how to do that." Remember, we want your child to feel ownership over the potty – "I run this show!" We want them to think, "This is my job and I've just given myself a promotion from diaper-wearer to potty-user!"

If jellybeans or stickers don't have a place in potty mastery, then what do you have left in your toolbox? Connection. Intention. Support. Encouragement. These are all powerful forces. They enable you to hold space for success and

celebration, rather than pressure and expectations. You can connect in the moment, regardless of what has or hasn't happened in the toilet. You can also reflect information about their efforts back to the child and provide them with the necessary encouragement they need for success.

Picture this: Your child has just peed in the potty for the first time. Some is on the floor, some is on the seat, some is sprinkled on their pants and, YES! Some is in the potty! They feel proud! You feel proud, too. You kneel on the floor, look into their face and say, "You did it! You listened to your body! You felt the need to pee, you ran to the potty, and you did your very best to get your pee in the potty. That's very important work!"

Everything in this statement is about your child's accomplishment. You did not say, *"I'm* so proud of you." That statement is about you. You shined the spotlight solely on your child. You celebrated their success. (You did it.) You used a technique from Conscious Discipline called "noticing," in which you described exactly what your child did to increase their body awareness. (You felt the need to pee, you ran to the potty, and you did your very best to get your pee in the potty.) And you made an encouraging statement about their effort. (That's very important work!) Encouraging the effort, as well as the outcome, helps children persist even though the outcome may not be perfect every time.

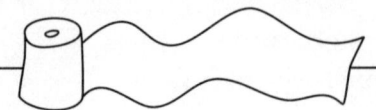

Noticing. Noticing is a basic Conscious Discipline strategy for offering encouragement and developing internal motivation. Research shows that effective feedback is accurate, specific, timely, non-judgmental and offered in the context of goals. Noticing meets all these criteria, and promotes eye contact, self-awareness and interpersonal connection. It is an optimal form of feedback that stimulates the brain, nourishes relationships, and sparks internal motivation.

The basic formula for noticing is: "You __(describe what they did)__ so __(describe why it was helpful)__" Then, instead of saying "good job," you can add a non-judgmental tag like, "You did it!" or "Way to go!"

Best of all, you can still use the power of noticing to highlight what your child is doing even when they aren't actually producing something in the potty. For example, "You walked into the bathroom, pushed down your pants and sat on the toilet. Hooray for you!" This helps to shift the adult's focus from the negative (what's not happening) to the positive (what is happening). Noticing in this way pivots the child's attention towards the desired behavior, increases their awareness and provides evidence of their growing success.

I do want to say, though, that my caution against rewards is not absolute. In fact, a small treat can sometimes be a helpful nudge along the path. Many children will feel frustrated or hesitant at some point in the potty mastery process. They may feel like giving up. You may feel like giving up. Sometimes, a little incentive is helpful for them, just like promising yourself a treat at the end of a long workday is helpful for you. There is a difference between relying on rewards in attempts to motivate a child, and using a special treat to celebrate or sustain momentum when the going gets tough. Go ahead and enjoy a special activity or a little treat once in a while. The key is to keep the focus on the inherent value of pottying, not the value of the prize. You can say, "You've been working so hard on pottying, let's celebrate all your successes this week with a special dance party. You pick the songs!"

Each time you reach out and shine that verbal light on your child's efforts, you're paying into their bank of inherent self-worth. You're reminding them that their actions are their own and that they are in control of their body. And that's a deposit of great value!

Why Is Potty Mastery Different?

Think about your child when they were a little baby. Squishy? Yes. Sweet-smelling? Yes. And you were so proud of them! Everything they did. You took photo after photo of that first smile. You felt pride and joy the first time they held their head up. You felt excited each time they did something new, even if they weren't completely successful. You praised them just for trying, even if it took weeks or months to accomplish the end goal.

So why do we so often perceive the potty differently? Let me offer some scenarios. See if any of them are familiar: Your baby rolls from front to back but can't quite go from back to front. You celebrate! They sit up for a minute, then fall to one side and smash their nose. You pick them up, kiss their booboo and shower them with praise. Or, all the time they spend rocking back and forth on all fours as they try to crawl. They're *almost* moving forward, so you cheer them on! What about when they take their first step and fall down immediately, but who cares?! You celebrate because they're *walking*! Your child notices they have to pee and races to the bathroom but doesn't quite make it to the potty. Do you celebrate the puddle just short of the toilet? Maybe yes, but also maybe no, right?

When it comes to the potty, parents often react with frustration, annoyance or even despair. Your child is right there, absorbing your reaction whether you say something outright or express it through nonverbal cues. (Young children are surprisingly adept at reading our nonverbal language and mood.) They're thinking, "I screwed up! Dad is mad. I did something wrong." Your child knows that their pottying matters to you. And they clearly know, but don't understand why all of a sudden they're being celebrated only for their successes, and not for trying. This is another way potty mastery is different from traditional potty *training*: We're going to focus on celebrating the attempts as well as the successes.

3
Gearing Up

Attempts matter to children. Their work right now is learning to take care of their own body, and using the potty is part of that work. Controlling their bowels and bladder is just one way children are trying to teach themselves to become more independent, which is a really, *really* important part of growing up!

As you're gearing up to start potty mastery, you'll want to begin laying the groundwork by reminding your child of all the important work they already do to take care of and listen to their bodies. This pre-work really can be a game-changer. In fact, it's hard to overstate the incredible importance of this early work! Noticing the many ways your child already takes care of their body will increase their awareness. Focusing on their efforts and offering guidance in an upbeat and encouraging way will help set them up for success.

"Wow," you might say to your child who asks for a snack, "You're listening to your body and your body's telling you it is hungry for something to eat."

 "Good for you," you might say when your child drenches the countertop while washing their hands, "You're taking care of your body by washing and drying your hands so they are clean! Now use a paper towel to dry off the countertop. Wiping up the water you splash is part of taking care of yourself, too!"

We are really focusing on two points:

1. Listening to your body is important
2. Taking care of your body is important.

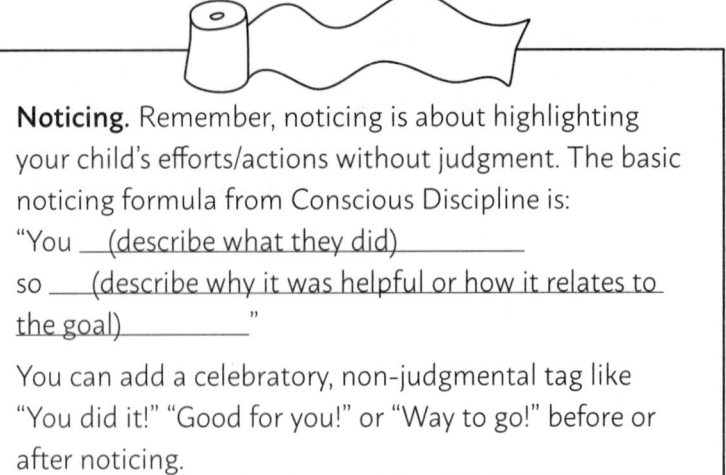

Noticing. Remember, noticing is about highlighting your child's efforts/actions without judgment. The basic noticing formula from Conscious Discipline is:
"You ___(describe what they did)___
so ___(describe why it was helpful or how it relates to the goal)___ "
You can add a celebratory, non-judgmental tag like "You did it!" "Good for you!" or "Way to go!" before or after noticing.

These are the two primary skills involved in potty mastery, and the first informs the second. Your child listens to their body so they can recognize the need to pee and poop. Your child takes care of their body by putting their pee and poop inside the potty. Your pre-work is to help your child feel like they already know how to listen to and take care of their body before they start using the potty. Every time they ask for something to eat or drink, remind them how well they listen to their body. Feel free to spell this out to your child directly by "noticing"– there's no hidden message here. When your child asks for a drink of water, you can say: "You're listening to your body. You're thirsty, so you asked for some water." This may feel a little obvious and a little clunky to you, but it won't to your child.

Highlight how well your child already takes care of their body. Every time your child washes their hands, bathes, eats healthy food or wears clean clothing, you can take a moment to connect that specific action to bodily care. Getting dressed is another important way to promote your child's self-care. You most likely don't want your child to just lie on the bed like a sardine while you wrestle them into their clothes, right? You'd like them to sit up, take their pants in their hands and try to puzzle out how to put them on. They might eventually get them on backwards, and it might take weeks to figure out the leg-holes, and even longer to figure out how to turn a sleeve right-side-out. Through it all, you will be providing encouragement, celebrating their efforts and helping them manage their frustration when the task feels overwhelming. You'll support their awareness with phrases like, "Look at you! You're dressing yourself! That's another important way to take care of your body!" Learning to dress themselves is a different form of self-care that also supports their autonomy. And, it will feel like an important accomplishment when they finally, FINALLY do it! The potty is going to be no different — a long, messy process and a key part of their developing independence.

You can also apply this "noticing" skill to your child's emotional state to increase their self-awareness and self-regulation skills. When your child comes to you crying, you can say, "Tears are coming from your eyes! You seem so sad. You listened to your body and came to me for comfort and help." Then hold your child and breathe together as you continue saying, "Breathe with me. You're safe."

All of this pre-work is important. Eventually, when you introduce potty mastery to your child, you'll be able to explain that using the potty is another important way for them to be in charge of their body. They get to *listen* to their body so they can recognize when they need to pee and poop. They get to *take care* of their body by putting their pee and poop in the potty. And because of all of the masterful pre-work you've put in, your child will think: *That's great because I already know how to listen and take care of my body!*

Remember, your primary job is to encourage your child's efforts, celebrate their incremental successes and help them manage their frustration when the task feels too big and overwhelming for them to manage—just like you've done with other skills like crawling, walking, feeding and dressing themselves.

Now let's shift over to a rather awkward conversation: How long has it been since *you've* pooped or peed in a diaper? Most likely, a long time. So long ago that you cannot remember what it was like. So let's take a short field trip into your child's mind to remind ourselves how different it is to poop in a diaper versus poop in the potty.

As a toddler, a diaper is always available. It is all you've ever known and it lives with you. Pooping and peeing are not actions that are separated from other parts of your day. You're not in charge of your diaper, it's your parent or your caregiver's responsibility. Nothing is asked of you during the diaper-changing process. And, as gross as it sounds, your poop and pee is held up against you. It's snuggled right up to you, and you've never known it any other way.

Now you're being asked to separate your poop and pee actions, and put them in a fixed place that doesn't follow you around—the potty. And that will feel a whole lot different and require a whole lot more effort than wearing a diaper!

It's also important to understand the emotional impact associated with un-diapering. For some children, transitioning from diapers to underpants will create feelings of loss. It's the loss of something that is known and familiar. It's the loss of the warmth that a wet and soiled diaper creates around a child's backside. It's the loss of the freedom to urinate and defecate wherever and whenever a child wants.

It's the loss of babyhood!

Even if your child doesn't experience feelings of loss, moving out of diapers and into underpants is a big transition. Transitions are tricky because things are in flux which can make them feel more uncertain and confusing. That's another reason why conflicting or ambivalent feelings are more likely to arise during potty learning.

Understanding your child's emotions and behaviors will help you connect with your child in a more authentic and supportive manner. When children feel heard and understood, they are better able to learn new skills, like using the potty!

Mastering the Potty

Potty mastery consists of two parts: A child's skill and a child's will. Let's look at both.

Skill. To begin to master the potty, your child will need to combine three specific skills: an intellectual understanding that pee and poop go into the potty, a realization of the feeling of needing to pee and poop, and a basic understanding of timing. Let's unpack each one.

Children learn the skill — the intellectual understanding that pee and poop go in the potty — on their own and usually from as early of an age as fifteen months. They begin to grasp the meaning as they watch the corresponding actions of the adults around them who say, "I'll be right there! I just need to go potty."

And think of all the times you've crammed yourself, a stroller, some shopping bags and a wide-eyed toddler into a bathroom stall with you. Pottying with an audience... Fun, isn't it? How about when your child narrates what you're doing for the listening pleasure of anyone else in the bathroom? "What's that?" "Are you wiping?" "Can I flush?"

Apart from being a super-fun, relaxing experience for you, this is also excellent education for your child. When you talk about the potty or let them watch you go to the potty, you're showing them just how and where the poop and pee go.

However, just because your child knows where it goes doesn't necessarily mean they know how to put their *own* poop or pee in the potty. For that, they'll need the next item on our skill list: the realization of the feeling of needing to poop and pee.

Babies start out unaware of the feeling of needing to poop and pee. As they mature into toddlerhood, they naturally become more aware of the feeling, especially the feeling of needing to poop. They might go behind the sofa to poop in their diaper, or squat down, or tell you not to look at them while they're pooping. These are signs that they're aware of their need to poop and that they're starting to separate out this task from other actions in their life.

Peeing is a little more difficult to monitor. We're often not actually sure when a child pees in their diaper during the day — dozens of times? A few times? Are they holding it or letting it dribble out? We usually only know that, at some point, their diaper has reached a level of noticeable wetness and so we change it. It's important to note that children may become aware of their need to poop and pee at different times.

Our goal is to help our children move from being unaware to becoming self-aware. This process involves children noticing the body sensations that signal their need to pee and poop and then planning their actions before the poop and pee come out. This is the essence of potty mastery. And this sort of time management doesn't come easily to children. Perhaps you've noticed that they're not particularly great at consciously stopping what they're doing (especially if it's fun) and beginning the process of going potty.

Now that we've talked through these three areas, you can probably see that potty mastery isn't just the process of onboarding three new skills; it is the process of integrating these new skills into one fluid action.

Will. When I say "will," I'm referring to a child's desire or willingness to put their pee and poop in the potty. It can be hard for your child to develop and maintain the will, or motivation, to keep up their potty mastery efforts. Supporting the process in ways that avoid power struggles, and recovering from them in a connected, compassionate manner when they *do* happen, will help keep your child moving steadily forward.

Power struggles happen when the adult's will and the child's will collide. They happen when you're trying to take over. The first step in avoiding power struggles is accepting that your child is in charge of their body; they are directing the show. When you attempt to assert control, you reduce their motivation. Stop insisting your child use the potty. Give the power over to your child and let them know you believe they can do this!

Another key to will and motivation is your connection with your child. Willingness goes hand-in-hand with connection. It's vitally important that you and your child maintain a healthy attachment during the potty mastery process. The two of you are a team. Let your child know that your relationship, your love, their worth and their value are not linked to their success or lack of  success using the potty. You're their pit crew; their support system. When your driver gets stuck, you're there to lend a hand. But it's not your race; it's theirs.

4
Readiness Signals

Is my child ready to use the potty? Let's be honest. This is probably one of the biggest questions you'd like an answer to right now. The other question might be, "Will my reluctant child ever be potty-trained?" To that one, I can easily say, "Yes, and not when they're fifteen, either!" To answer, "Is my child ready?" you'll need to do a bit of check-in with both yourself and your child.

I've found that parents usually think of this scenario when they picture potty-readiness: your child asks you to take off their diaper. Then they run to the potty and they sit down. Viola! The pee is in the potty! Maybe a little gets on the floor, but who cares? They do this most times, most days, with the occasional accident along the way, and with only a fraction of the number of peed-in diapers of previous weeks. That's it, right? Your child is signaling that they're ready for the potty.

If only the signal was that clear. For the majority of households, that scene tends to exist in the realm of the imagination. It sounds great, but in reality, the signals that your child is ready for the potty are a little messier and a lot more subtle.

Behavior Signals

We've already discussed one signal: a child who regularly disappears behind the couch to go poop in their diaper and asks you to change it after they've pooped in it. What other signs can we look for to signal a child is ready for potty mastery?

Do they try to get themselves dressed? I don't mean, "Do they reliably put on all their clothes correctly and without help?" You'd never leave the house! What I'm talking about is whether your child is *trying* to put on some of their own clothes, even if they put their feet in the armholes of their shirt. Showing a desire to dress and undress themselves is an important potty-readiness step. It's another way your child is demonstrating self-care: I know I can put on my clothes; I know I can take care of my body.

Perhaps your child pulls at their wet or dirty diaper. This often means they're aware they've urinated or defecated and that they'd like their dirty diaper removed because it feels more comfortable to be clean or dry.

Another readiness sign could be a child's interest in other people's toileting. Does your child frequently say, "I hear your pee-pee going in the toilet," or "Can I watch you poop?" Maybe they mimic you by sitting on the toilet even when they are not yet aware of their body signals. Your child is letting you know that they are observing the toileting process and trying to make sense of it on their own.

How about children who use potty talk — "doodoo," "poopy butt," "butthole" as they gleefully riff about pee and poop. Fear not! Although these comments may sound off-putting, remember a pre-potty child has no sense of decorum and using potty talk can go hand-in-hand with their piqued interest in potty learning.

Or perhaps your child routinely tells you they are about to pee and poop, even if they are reluctant to use the unfamiliar potty. They are demonstrating that they are able to attune to their body signals, which is an important part of mastering the potty.

Signs to Look for During Play

What about making connections and associations when playing with toys? Does your child pretend to cook with pots and a spatula in the play kitchen? Do they drive the cars into the toy garage and line them up in the parking spaces? Does your child put their stuffed animal to bed and cover them tenderly with a blanket? If your child's imaginative play regularly has them creating scenarios in which their toys do things  in locations that are specific to their function, they'll likely be able to connect that pee and poop belong in a special place, too – the potty.

Perhaps they don't play with toys like this. Maybe they still like motor-driven play: opening and shutting, dumping and filling, pushing and pulling, and putting things in and out of other things. That's excellent, important play. It shows that your child is focused on motor movement. Good! They need these skills. But they might not be quite ready for potty mastery if this is their main type of play. Wait until they start making meaningful connections when playing with their toys before you start the potty mastery process.

Communication Skills

Another important signal of potty readiness is your child's ability and willingness to communicate, either verbally or non-verbally, the need to use the potty. Both of these aspects are important: *can* your child communicate their need to use the potty and *will* they communicate the need to use the potty?

Your child can communicate with you, the parent, of course. But if they go to preschool, they also need to feel comfortable communicating with the adults and teachers there. Sometimes, you might need to think creatively. I once worked with a family whose child spoke very little at school, but she still needed a way to communicate her toilet needs. So, we made a plan together: we placed a picture of a potty in an obvious spot in the classroom. When the child needed to go, she pointed to the picture. Communication achieved!

Some children are much more cautious or reserved than others, especially at school. That's okay. These children just may need some coaching or practice from you in order to learn how to communicate their potty needs. You know your child best, so you and your child's preschool will want to put on your creative thinking caps to find a workable solution together.

When assessing your child's potty readiness, try not to focus on the amount of functional skill that is already in place. Think of the child's ability and willingness to learn. Instead of asking yourself, "Is my child ready to use the potty?" try asking, "Is my child *capable of learning* this new skill?" As with many questions in this book, there's no right or wrong answer. There is only the answer that describes your child at this moment in time.

Adult Signals

Are you ready for your child to give up diapers... Two and a half years of nonstop, 24-hour diaper changes... Pinning a wiggling toddler down in the back of a minivan in a parking lot while you insist that they cannot hold their poopy diaper while they insist otherwise... Diapers, wipes and cream filling your shopping cart and draining your bank account over and over again like some cruel version of *Groundhog Day*, only with Pampers in the starring role instead of Bill Murray... Of course you're ready!

But do you know your job and are you committed to it? Accurately assessing *your* job and fully committing to your job will help your child do their job. The overarching task you'll need to remember is that your child's worth and value are not linked to their success or lack of success on the potty. You know this, of course, but it's surprisingly easy to forget when they've flooded the floor. Again. As I mentioned earlier, your encouragement and your fundamental belief in your child's worthiness, regardless of their potty success, will help sustain their willingness to achieve this milestone. Communicating to your child that they're lovable, valuable and worthy *no matter what* is absolutely essential to their confidence and success during potty learning.

Remember when we discussed how important it is for a child to practice self-care? It's important for parents to care for themselves, too. This means protecting your psyche. Potty mastery is going to be a process. It might feel uncomfortable for you as it brings up unconscious wounds from your childhood or tests your modern-day frustration tolerance. Some solid self-care is going to be essential to your wellbeing. Remind yourself (possibly several times a day) that your self-worth and success as a parent does not hinge on whether your child successfully uses the potty. Connecting your worth to your child's potty mastery is a sign that you're taking ownership of the potty-process. Remember, this is your child's job, not yours. You can't make a child go to the potty.

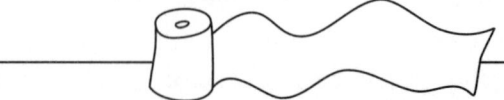

As they say in Conscious Discipline, "**Q**uit **T**aking **I**t **P**ersonally (Q.T.I.P.)." It isn't happening to you, it's happening in front of you. It isn't about you, it's about their learning experience. Their job is to master the potty. Your job is to lovingly support and encourage them.

Staying calm and composed even when the process is going slowly and in the face of setbacks is your top priority. Managing your feelings—whether excitement, anger, weariness, frustration or other—will help keep the focus where it belongs: on the child. Your child won't be wasting energy trying to read your face. Instead of wondering if they're pleasing Daddy or if Mommy's angry they wet the floor, your child can focus on their own very important job of potty mastery. If you remain calm and believe your child can do this (and they definitely can), then you'll communicate this belief to your child through your energy, actions and words.

If you're feeling discouraged, remind yourself that it's absolutely, positively, 100% normal to have strong feelings related to your child's potty mastery progress (or lack thereof). It's also your job to manage your feelings so you can be the calm, supportive assistant they need. It can help to plan a pep talk or mantra for yourself that you can repeat to remind yourself that your child is working hard to learn a new skill and that this phase won't last forever.

From Dr. Bailey: My granddaughters are as smart as they are determined, but even they had many stops and starts on their pottying journeys. As each girl's unique process unfolded, I'd encourage their mom, "She's got her own timeline, but she'll get there." Believing in a child's potential, especially in the face of inconsistent progress, is empowering! What we think about others impacts how we perceive them *and* their actual behavior.

Few of us can pick up a new skill successfully on the first try. Think about how long it took you to learn a recent skill, and how much trial and error, experimentation and guidance it took. Potty mastery is the same for your child. And learning a new skill, well, it can be exhausting. You (and your child) might even feel like giving up, 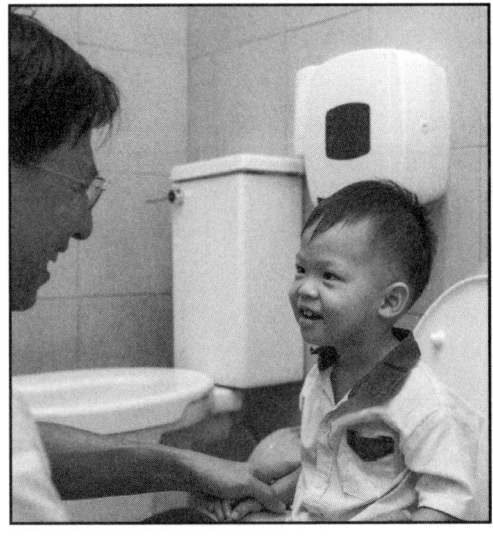 especially when little Oliver from next door is zooming around in his superhero underpants with no puddles in sight. Don't despair. Your child will learn the potty. And you *will* help.

This chart can help, if your brain could use a little rearranging:

Adult Perception	If you find yourself thinking:	Make a shift by telling yourself:
Getting started	I'm going to make my child use the potty.	I'm going to support and encourage my child in learning to use the potty.
	How do I get my child to use the potty?	How can I help my child be successful in learning to use the potty?
Child is showing slow progress	There's something wrong with my child.	My child needs a little more time to make these connections.
	I'm doing all the work here. They're just not trying hard enough!	This is my child's journey, not mine. They need a little more time to make these connections.
Child has frequent accidents	This is making me miserable!	This isn't about me; it's about my child and I know they can do it.
	I can't possibly clean another pair of underwear or go over the potty routine with them *again*!	My child is working hard to figure this out. They will get there.
	I'm not doing this anymore! I quit!	I have a choice. I can continue working with my child or I can put potty mastery on pause for a while. Which is healthiest for my family right now?

The Skill of Composure. Conscious Discipline is organized around the Seven Powers of Conscious Adults and Seven Skills of Discipline. The Powers are perceptual shifts. The Skills are the strategies that stem from the Powers. Composure is central to your child's potty mastery experience. It stems from the Power of Perception, which reminds us that we have a choice about how to see events. Whether we see a child's behavior as a call for help or a sign of failure will aid or derail our ability to remain composed during potty mastery.

Choosing a helpful perception allows us to access the higher centers of our brain so we can respond to frustrations and missteps with wisdom. Taking three deep belly breaths, repeating a reassuring mantra ("I'm safe. I can handle this. Keep breathing.") and choosing to focus on the positive (the behaviors we want to see) are all helpful for maintaining our composure during potty mastery.

Accepting Accidents

Accidents are going to happen, no matter what. Even the most skilled potty master is going to occasionally miscalculate. Accidents can be incredibly frustrating – they're messy, smelly, time-consuming and not very fun to clean up. There are few things less pleasurable than scrubbing out poopy underwear, no matter how much you love the person wearing them.

Accepting that accidents are inevitable and then managing your feelings when they do happen is another key element of parent potty readiness. In fact, I'm going to go even further and say that accidents are not only inevitable, they are a necessary and helpful part of the learning process. We're accustomed to thinking of accidents as exclusively negative. But actually, each accident is a chance for your child to learn. This might require a bit of a mindset shift.

Each time your child wets or dirties their underwear, they can feel it. They can smell it. The poop and pee evidence are right in front of them. They can experience, in real time, the discomfort of wet and dirty versus the comfort of clean and dry.

Parents will usually go to great lengths to keep a child from having an accident. Imagine a parent whisking a child from a room, pulling down their pants and physically placing them on the potty. The message is pretty clear. Accidents = bad. No accidents = good.

I suggest we throw out that equation. When parents direct all their energy at avoiding accidents, we are basically acting as an action-oriented, parent-shaped diaper. It's another way of making potty mastery the parent's job. And of course, it really is the child's job. The immediate physical feedback of an accident tells your child in no uncertain terms that they cut it too close, that they missed their body's early cues, that they need to allow extra time when they're wearing overalls or playing outside, etc. When we whisk them off, speedily undress them and plop them on the potty, we save our children from the natural consequence of their actions (or lack thereof). Natural consequences are the most powerful motivators for behavioral change. They're our friend, not our enemy. Our job is to peacefully let them happen, and gently guide the child through their disappointment and into self-reflection so they can understand on a deep level how and why to do it differently next time.

Natural Consequences. Natural consequences occur organically as the result of our action (or inaction), and are one of the most effective motivators for change. A child who feels the natural consequence of discomfort from grabbing a hot pan becomes *highly* motivated to check the temperature more cautiously next time. A child who feels the discomfort from wet underwear and the corresponding clean-up becomes more motivated to act more quickly the next time they feel the urge to use the toilet. As the parent, you don't have to do anything or say anything, simply support and empathize with your child as their inherent discomfort motivates the change.

Of course, you're likely not a Zen master; you're likely a busy person whose life often feels like a complex balancing act. Choosing to see a puddle on the floor as a learning opportunity might be extremely difficult. I get it. I'm not advocating for you to *love* accidents. And I'm not advocating for your child to have one in aisle 5 at the  grocery store or on the dance floor at Aunt Kim's wedding. I *am* asking you to practice being an "accidents-are-a-part-of-learning" Zen master by letting accidents happen when possible and appropriate, and then handling them with empathy and grace. I think we can all agree there's a big difference between an accident in the backyard versus an accident captured by a wedding photographer. The point is that choosing to perceive accidents as learning opportunities removes the stigma and shame from them when they do happen, and allows for a massive dose of motivation and self-education through natural consequences. Try to befriend your child's accidents, even if you're not quite ready to be BFFs.

5
Preparation

You're helping your child listen to their body when they're hungry or thirsty, so they become aware of the signals their body sends. You're encouraging your child to dress more independently and brush their own teeth, so they begin to see that caring for their body is their own job. Your  child is making connections and associations when playing with their toys. You're studying your own mindset and noticing your own feelings so you become self-aware and are able to remain calm, even in the face of accidents.

So let's discuss another absolutely key element to potty mastery: a parent's language. Your words matter. Most children are learning to use the potty sometime during their second year of life. What's happening inside a two-year-old, developmentally? It's a big tug-of-war: I want to be a baby. I am a baby. I want to be a big kid. I *am* a big kid.

This struggle is normal and necessary. But we don't need to exacerbate it with the language traditionally used during potty learning. Let's picture a pretty ordinary scene.

You're driving with your child — always a good time for conversation. The subject of the potty comes up and casually you say, "You're such a big kid! That's why you get to use the potty!" Or alternately, you might come out with, "You're going to wear big kid underwear because you're growing up and getting so big!"

Well, maybe your child doesn't feel like being big or growing up right now. Maybe they're feeling like they want to be a baby at that moment. That's fine, but you've just told them that "big" is good and "big" is linked to the potty. Not so helpful to the pottying process for someone who wants to be a baby at that moment.

If it's counter-productive to tell a child how great it is to be big and go pee on the potty, then what the heck do we say?

A lot, as it turns out. It's time to reframe the potty dialogue. Instead of focusing the conversation around how big and mature and grown-up your child is, we're going to talk about your child's *job* instead. Their job regarding potty mastery is being in charge of their own body. And you *know* how much children love to be in charge! Most parents live that reality every day.

Children also love the idea of jobs. They're familiar with jobs; all the important people in their lives have them. And these are the people they most want to be like. Folding clothes, washing tables, sweeping the floor— they're eager to be a part of the adult world, and that world often means the world of work. So,

telling your child that they're going to soon have a job will have them sitting up and paying attention fast.

Your Child's New Job: Becoming a Body Boss

During a relaxing moment in your day, maybe cuddling together before nap or after reading a book, tell your child that soon they will have a big, important job:

Say: "You will become a Body Boss and you will be in charge of your body."

Explain: "A Body Boss *listens* to their *body* so they can recognize when they need to pee and poop. And a Body Boss *takes care of their body* by putting their pee and poop inside the potty." (If you did your pre-work by encouraging your child to listen and take care of their body, this language will sound familiar and comfortable.)

Remind your child: "Being a Body Boss is so awesome and cool, and the only one who can do it is you!" (Remind yourself of this as well. Your child is in charge.)

Setting Up for Success

Start your potty mastery process during a time when you and your child will be home for a few days. A long weekend is ideal. Try to pick a time that's relatively stress-free or at least free of major transitions such as the weeks before or after the birth of a new baby, house guests, starting a new childcare placement, a family vacation or a move to a new house, just to name a few.

Plan to take care of the potty process at home, not at school. Your child will need an attentive adult and a safe, secure, peaceful place when they initially start learning about the potty. After a few days of practicing at home, your child will be better prepared to bring their potty learning into their childcare setting. Make sure to consult with your child's preschool teacher or childcare leader before launching the process since it can be very challenging when multiple children from the same class are in the early stages of potty learning at the same time.

Play Props

When we think of potty props, most of us immediately think of potty books. You may already have a shiny stack of them beside your child's bed, all ready for reading. Excellent. Potty books are a great tool for your child's new job.

But *play* is how children learn best and come to understand their world. Adding some potty props into your child's imaginative play will help your child figure out their feelings about the potty and how they're going to tackle problems. Props can also help them play-practice these new skills, which can be especially helpful if the going gets rough. Learning new skills like peeing and pooping in the potty can feel stressful for children, just like learning something new at work can feel stressful for you. Playing with potty props and acting out their experiences are problem solving mechanisms and stress relief valves for your child. They help them feel safe while they make sense of the important new skills they're learning.

Consider identifying a doll or a stuffed animal that can learn about the potty along with your child. There are dozens of diaper-clad dolls meant to do their business in the diaper, but you'll need to improvise when it comes to a doll or stuffy who's learning to use the potty. See if you can find a doll-sized potty or potty chair. Maybe the doll or animal can wear a pair of underpants. Set up a little area of your child's play space with a small laundry basket, a washer and dryer made out of boxes, a potty and some toilet paper. Then step back and let your child make this their world.

It's tempting to set up the potty props, including the potty, before your child is ready to start playing with them. Many parents do this thinking the early exposure will be helpful. I don't recommend this because I've found that the opposite is often true. Exposing your child to the potty props and potty chair too early can actually get in the way of their success.

Children want power and control – this is important to remember. Children can get confused if you make the potty optional at first ("Here's the potty. You can use it if you want, and if you don't want to, that's fine too"), and then change your tune later ("You need to use the potty all the time"). First you said one thing and now you're saying another. Children usually meet confusion with resistance. This leads to power struggles, which you want to avoid above all else.

More than that, children – like most people – don't like having their choices taken away. Using the potty is your child's job. Consider your own job. Imagine for a moment your boss giving you an assignment that was optional at first. But then, on an arbitrary date, your boss decided you'd be doing that assignment all the time. Would you be pleased and happy or annoyed and tempted to argue? When you give your child a choice and then take it away, you also take away your child's power and autonomy.

It's also helpful to preserve as much novelty as possible during the potty mastery process. Putting out the potty props too early kills the novelty. Children are naturally curious and love to figure out how things work. When something is brand-new, they get excited and interested. It captures their attention and they want to explore and examine it. But after a while, the curiosity wears off, especially if something is sitting around for a long time without being used. If you aren't intentional about using the potty props because it's not time to start the process yet, children naturally begin to lose interest. The potty props become familiar objects, like any other object in the house, and it will be harder to draw the child's interest back to them when it's time to start the potty process in earnest.

Prepping the Bathroom

Of course, this is where the magic is going to happen – or at least where you *hope* the magic is going to happen. Take some time to make the bathroom a really pleasant, welcoming space for your child. After all, you two are going to be spending quite a bit of time in there together.

If you can, try to have both a separate potty chair and also an insert for the adult toilet. Some children prefer one, some like the other. Who doesn't like options? Offer both, if possible.

A stepstool placed under the big toilet is a very important item many parents overlook. This stool should be high enough that your child can firmly plant their feet on it.

They'll need to bear down to have a bowel movement (think of yourself and you'll understand) and this stool will help them activate the right muscles.

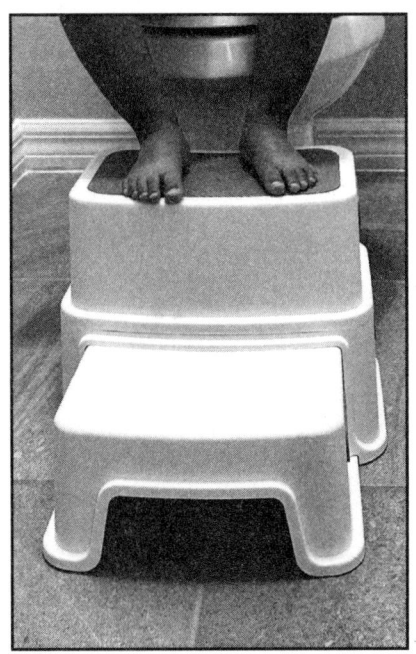

After you've gotten a potty chair, a potty insert and a sturdy step stool, take a little field trip back into your child's bedroom. Look around. Is there a changing table or pad lurking in the corner? Now's the time to do a little decluttering.

Haul that changing table out to the curb, up to the attic or down the street to your pregnant neighbor's house. You want to send a message to your child: All toilet activities now occur in that amazing sanctuary known as the bathroom. No one's changing diapers in the bedroom anymore. Remove all signs of diapering- tubs of cream, random wipes and cloths, and all those squished up bottles and tubes on the changing table. Take it all to the bathroom. You're sending a clear message: "The bathroom is where poop and pee activities happen."

Visual Routines

As an adult, you have a voice in your head that helps you make decisions and governs your behaviors. Because young children lack inner speech, they often need concrete images in order to understand what comes next and determine whether or not it's safe to do something. The more visual images children see, the easier it is for them to understand what's expected.

Your day is filled with routines—things you do the same way day, after day, after day. These routines are often ingrained in our experiences, but they may not be so clear to children. For children to be successful, they need to know what success looks like. Visual routines show children exactly what to do and in what order. Common children's routines include teeth brushing, dressing, getting out of the house, bedtime, hand washing and, yes, going potty. If any of these activities are frequent trouble-spots, then posting a visual routine can cultivate success. The Conscious Discipline website has extensive video tutorials and other resources to help you understand and create visual routines.

Autonomous toileting requires nine specific steps. Nine steps are a lot! Because a young child's brain is only primed for a few instructions at a time, it's helpful to separate the potty routine into three shorter sequences:

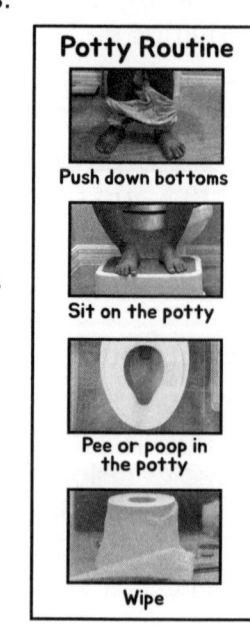

Potty Routine

Push down bottoms

Sit on the potty

Pee or poop in the potty

Wipe

1. Pre-Potty:
   • Feel the urge to potty.
   • Walk to the bathroom.

2. Potty:
   • Push down bottoms and underwear.
   • Sit on the potty.
   • Put pee and poop in the potty.
   • Wipe.

3. Post-Potty:
   • Pull up bottoms.
   • Flush.
   • Wash and dry hands.

The first two sequences may seem simple on the surface, but this is where children do most of the work. When we take a moment to put ourselves in a child's shoes, it's easy to see how these two sequences require children to shift from carefree poops and pees *anywhere*, to noticing the urge far enough in advance that they can make it to the toilet, take their bottoms down and sit on the toilet in time to do their business. There's a lot of finesse and hard work involved in accomplishing these steps!

Self-care is an inherent part of potty learning. You can decide whether you will initially help your child wipe and later transition them to independent wiping, or if your child will do it independently from the beginning. Your decision should consider your child's temperament and your attunement to what feels most comfortable for them. If your child is slow to warm up, they may benefit from your assistance. If they are strong-willed and determined, put them in charge. Remember, there is no right or wrong way, only what feels right for your child. Whichever option you choose, show it in your visual routine.

The same principle holds true for boys with sitting vs standing. Generally speaking, most boys begin the potty mastery process by sitting on the potty to urinate and defecate. It simplifies their learning. But this is usually a temporary situation. As soon as little boys figure out that they can stand and urinate, they often easily (and willingly) transition to this position. Again, you know your child best. There is no right or wrong way to begin.

While visual routines that include photos of your own child demonstrating the steps for the three potty routine is ideal, creating them can feel daunting. Scan this QR code or go to https://consciousdiscipline.com/ free-resources/ to download and print premade pre-potty, potty and post-potty visual routines.

As you prepare your child for potty mastery— about the same time you introduce the potty play props— consider having a special photo session so you can feature your child in their visual potty routine. This is a wonderful opportunity to talk with your child about becoming a Body Boss as you discuss and role-play the potty routine. It's also an opportunity for you and your child to connect, so make the experience light-hearted and convey confidence in your child's ability to succeed. Don't hesitate to be silly or over-the-top with your photo-taking if your child responds well to that kind of play. Potty mastery is serious work, but it can be fun too!

Once you have taken the photos, it's time to print and post them in the appropriate location where your child will be doing that routine.

- Pre-Potty Routine: Child's bedroom or the family room (the living space where your child spends most of their time playing).
- Potty Routine: Bathroom near the toilet.
- Post-Potty Routine: Near the sink.

Although your visual routines will not make your house beautiful; they're temporary. You can remove each visual routine once your child is proficient at using it. The pre-potty routine will likely go away after a few weeks. The hand-washing part of your post-potty routine may be there indefinitely. (Those signs in the public restrooms are there for a reason!)

You may choose to remove the visual routines once your child is consistently successful. You can always re-post them later if your child regresses, which is exceedingly common and normal.

Undies! Undies! Undies!

A lot of parents go into potty mastery already armed with a drawer full of underwear. It seems like an obvious thing to stock up on as your child approaches the age of pottying. You may have bought this underwear a long time ago and without your child's involvement.

If possible, take your child on a ceremonial trip to the store anyway. Let them pick out a pack of underwear all on their own. This sends a message that supports body autonomy and agency: *"You are in charge of your body. You own the potty process.*

You are in charge of what you put on your body and what you do with the potty."

While you're wandering up and down the underwear aisle, you may encounter packs of "training pants" – thick, absorbent underwear meant to mop up leaks and spills. Don't let yourself get sucked in by that thick cotton. When learning the potty, you want your child to feel wet when they're wet. Feeling wetness is good. It provides an excellent contrast to what we're aiming for – dryness. If your child pees in training pants and all that excellent cotton just soaks up the pee, what signals does that give them about their body? What have they learned? Not a whole heck of a lot.

Naked Weekend

Underpants are an important part of being a Body Boss, but holding off on underwear for a short period of time can sometimes be helpful. Letting your child go naked from the waist down may help your child become more aware of what's going on inside and outside of their body. (Obviously, this is an at-home only activity, and it's not something all families would benefit from or are comfortable with.) Some parents jokingly call it "naked weekend," but it's no joke! Accidents and attempts will be very obvious to both them and you (yay!), and allow you to reinforce the goals: pee and poop out of the body. Pee and poop in the potty. However, caution is needed. For some children, the absence of a barrier like underpants will feel unsafe and may cause them to withhold. If your child feels more secure in underpants, provide them with underpants. If they're fine romping around the house without bottoms, simply keep their pants or shorts off while you are at home for those first few days. Use your innate understanding of your child to guide which approach will work best.

Cloth diapers and potty mastery: Some families use cloth diapers from infancy. Children who wear cloth diapers often attune to their body signals with greater ease because the cloth barrier is less absorbent than synthetic ones, so cloth diaper wearers *feel* wet. That's important biofeedback, especially for children for whom body awareness is challenging. However, cloth diapers are unlikely to help children who are apprehensive about the pottying process because they do not address the child's underlying concerns.

What About Staying Dry at Night?

The potty mastery process that we've walked through in this book is based on children's body awareness when they are awake. A child's ability to stay dry while they are sleeping often occurs at a later time. In fact, it may take a few additional months, or even a few additional years, before your child's able to remain dry both during the day and at night. Naptime dryness typically precedes nighttime dryness and I recommend looking for five consecutive days of dryness before your child transitions to underpants for sleeping.

Our "Body Boss" language works perfectly in terms of daytime and nighttime dryness. Just let your child know that when they are sleeping, they're off the job – just like parents are off the job when they're sleeping. You can remind your child that as their body grows and matures, they won't need diapers at naptime and bedtime anymore.

You can make this discussion more "real" for your child by creating a fun art project to do together. Get a box and let your child decorate it, with your help. Then label the box with your child's name and the words "Sleeping Diapers." Explain to your child that they are going to wear underpants when they're awake and diapers when they're asleep. Their diapers will remain in the *Sleeping Diapers* box. This box accomplishes three important objectives: It engages children's active participation. It helps to prepare children for their diaper-to-underpants transition. And it visually reminds children that they're off the job when they are asleep.

6
Launching

I've taught my Potty Mastery class to hundreds of parents over the years. And they've asked me over and over again, "How do I prepare my child for the actual transition?" Initially, I developed a system that worked pretty well. Two days in advance of the official No-Diapers Date, parents have the "Body Boss" conversation. Then, they hold up a small stack of diapers that are projected to last two days. Every time they change a diaper, they count the ever-smaller stack. Then, the night before the actual Body Boss transition, they point out that only one diaper is left. They remind their child that in the morning the new job begins. They become a Body Boss and they get to wear their new uniform... underpants!

This "stack of diapers" system is a good one and I still share it with parents. But it involves a lot of talking at children— a sure way to lose a child's attention and interest! For some children, the counting down may also 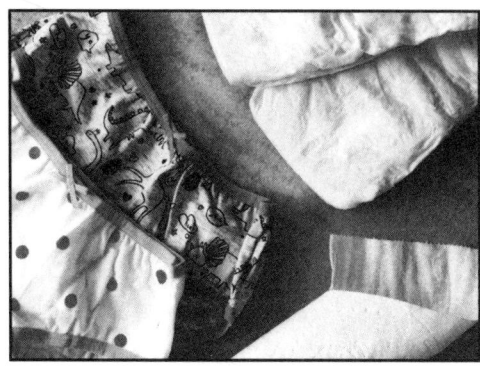 increase their anxiety rather than build excitement. As time passed, I realized children could be better prepared for this change with a ritual that grabbed their attention, encouraged them to get involved and tickled their curiosity.

I created the book *Diaper Doggie* to be enjoyed as part of a potty mastery ritual. The main character in the story is a warm, endearing pup who collects diapers from children who are preparing to become a Body Boss. Diaper Doggie, is on a very important mission. And best of all, Diaper Doggie gets kids involved, which is why this ritual works so well. Read the book in a calm and relaxed manner a few days leading up to the transition. The day before that transition, read the book once again. Next, help your child to collect their diapers. Together, leave them at their bedside before they go to sleep that evening. During the night, Diaper Doggie (that's you) collects the diapers and leaves behind a brand-new pair of underpants. When your child wakes up in the morning, they find their new underpants, they put them on – and they're off! To learn more about this book and purchase it go to www.parentstride.com.

You can, of course, create a similar ritual of your own without my book. The hallmarks of a meaningful ritual are eye contact, touch, presence and playfulness. Incorporate these factors if you choose to create your own undiapering ritual. Retell your story a few times before the transition commences.

The key points are as follows:

1. It's almost time to become a Body Boss.
2. Gather up the diapers, and put them in a bag beside your bed.
3. Your diapers will be replaced with underpants.
4. Put on the underpants in the morning.
5. It's time to start your new job:
     a.) Listen to your body so you notice when you need to poop and pee.
     b.) Take care of your body by putting your poop and pee in the potty.
6. New jobs take time to learn. Accidents happen and they help you learn!
7. I will encourage you each step of the way.
8. Soon you will become diaper-free!

Rituals: Authentic connection bonds us together and insulates us from the ill effects of stress. In her book *I Love You Rituals*, Dr. Becky Bailey discusses the four components needed for authentic connection—eye contact, touch, presence and a playful situation—and provides 75 quick activities that increase connection. During connecting rituals, your child is the center of your world and you are the center of theirs. Connecting rituals are like mini tune-ups for your child's emotional and physical wellbeing (and yours, too). Creating rituals containing these four components and building them into your potty toolbox will increase connection, cooperation and focus while decreasing any stressors associated with potty learning.

You'll know which rituals feel like a good fit for you and your child. Don't hesitate to add another layer of connection to commemorate the occasion and provide encouragement. You might create a special potty handshake or a short un-

diapering dance to symbolize your child's new learning and your commitment as their support person. Do the handshake or dance together before bed, at wakeup and after every potty attempt (whether successful or not). Use the handshake or dance to send the message "you can do it" as your child ventures out into the world without a diaper. Have fun and connect! The eye contact, touch, presence and playfulness you and your child share will trigger the brain to release the body's natural feel-good chemicals, bringing love, lightness and positivity into what can sometimes feel like a stressful process.

Language to Use During the Process

Does this sound familiar?

An earnest parent observes a dancing, squirming child: "Sweetie, do you need to go potty?"
Child, emphatically: "No!"

Children are masters of "the art of the no." Instead of relying on questions, utilize the skill of noticing to build the child's awareness of their body signals. "Your body's squirming like this..." *(Demonstrate.)* "Check in with your body. What is it saying?"

Or "Your body's squirming like this..." *(Demonstrate.)* "Seems like something's up! What do you think your body's trying to tell you?"

Notice their behavior, allow them to process your observation, and then wait for an answer before rushing them to the bathroom as a foregone conclusion. Remember, our goal is *not* to avoid accidents. Our goal is to help our children to build the body awareness needed to make it to the bathroom independently. Your child must learn to recognize the signals inside their body. An accident is a powerful natural consequence and important learning experience. Avoidance is a short-game technique; we're playing the long game.

Of course, sometimes it's important to guide them to use the potty, like when you're facing a long car ride. In that case, assertively say, "It's time to use the potty now" and provide a brief explanation. For example, "It's time to use the potty now. We're going on a long drive and there won't be many places to stop." Use this call to action sparingly. Our goal is for your child to develop their own potty-forecasting skills and make bathroom decisions for themselves the vast majority of the time.

Often with potty mastery, parents' language veers toward the negative. Conscious Discipline teaches that our language and intent shine a proverbial flashlight on our children's world, illuminating that which we value. When *we* focus on what they've done wrong or are not doing, we also focus *their* attention on the mistake. If they are focused on mistakes, they are not focused on improvement and solutions. Yes, you're going to acknowledge their oops, but the real power comes from shining your light frequently and consistently on what they're doing well. Instead of harping on them for missing the toilet again, verbalize how they noticed their body's potty signals, they made a beeline for the toilet and they were so close to making it. Surround them with information about what they did well and envelop them in the confidence that they can use what they've learned from their oops to be successful next time. It doesn't matter if it's their 100th oops this week; persist in your role as their #1 supporter.

Even when your child's progress seems agonizingly slow, it's still progress. For instance, if they sit and don't produce — they're practicing how to use the potty. If they try to make it to the potty and don't, well, then they recognized their body's signals. Their timing was just off. If they report they've had an accident, hooray! They know they need to take care of their body by putting on clean clothes. Reframing each misstep or accident as progress can be a morale boost for you as well as an important awareness and confidence-building opportunity for your child.

Intent Matters

Children may feel conflicted about using the potty. They're figuring out how to give up something that is comfortable and familiar, and work towards something that feels new, strange, inconvenient and unfamiliar. They're facing a trial-and-error learning process in which they will be dealing with the big feelings that often accompany mistakes... most likely a lot of mistakes and a lot of big feelings.

We don't want to contribute to this internal tug-of-war, yet we often do through our own inability to self-regulate. Blaming, shaming, pushing and insisting are signs of a dysregulated adult, which can derail the process and lead your child to feeling more conflicted. Our intent matters.

Our ability to self-regulate matters. Our children will feel it if we enter the process with an air of confidence and compassion versus one of impatience or frustration. Noticing our own uncomfortable sensations gives us important information that we've been triggered. From this state of self-awareness, we can re-center ourselves in order to create a warm, loving and encouraging presence. (It is also important to acknowledge that we are going to oops in our intent and language on occasion; when this happens, we can learn from our missteps just as we're hoping our children will learn from theirs.)

The more emotionally self-aware we become, the more attuned and responsive we become to our children's emotional experience. Failing to do this can cause children to experience feelings of shame and unworthiness, and further impede their willingness to move forward with their potty learning.

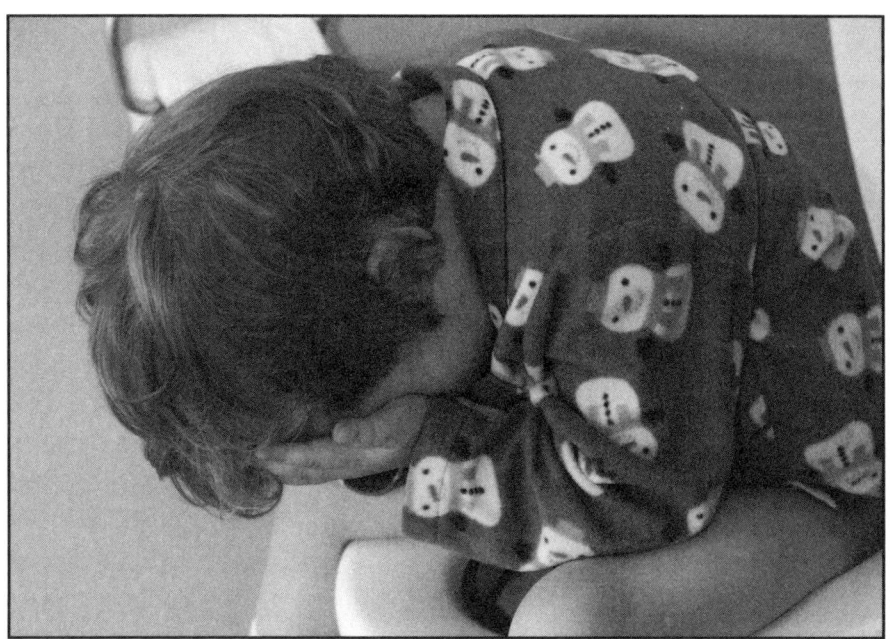

The following chart provides some helpful phrases to help you cultivate and convey positive intent during potty learning.

If Your Child	Avoid Saying	Instead Try
Has an accident	Did you pee in your pants?	Oops! You had an accident. Underpants are for keeping clean and dry. You are in charge of your body, so it's important to put on clean clothes. I can help if you'd like.
Must use the potty due to time-constraints	I need you to go potty.	It's important to use the potty now. You can use the big potty or the little potty. Which do you choose? (Two positive choices provide a degree of freedom while encouraging compliance.)
Is doing the potty dance	Do you need to use the potty?	"Your body's squirming like this..." (demonstrate) "Seems like something's up! What do you think your body's trying to tell you?" If this doesn't work, try reporting it: "Your body is squirming like this ... (demonstrate.) Your body is letting you know there's pee (or poop) that's ready to come out.

If Your Child	Avoid Saying	Instead Try
Has successfully used the potty	I'm so proud of you.	You did it! You felt the need to use the potty, went straight to the bathroom, pulled down your bottoms, sat on the toilet and went potty. Way to go!
Is resisting underwear	Don't you want to be a big kid?	You were hoping to wear diapers instead of underwear. That's what you were used to. You're learning to put your poop and pee in the potty now. To do that, you'll need underwear.
Is sitting on the potty but isn't going potty.	Go poopy for Mommy!	You are in charge of your body. Breathe with me so you can relax and check in with your body. (Take a deep breath together.) If your body's saying it's not ready yet, you can try again later.

In general, we want to avoid sending children messages that judge, including questions that have a "good" choice and a "bad" choice. References to underpants being for big kids or diapers being for babies is pretty loaded language. You're assigning a positive value to underpants (big kid) and a negative value to diapers (babyish). That's going to feel confusing at best, and personally insulting at worst.

Instead, offer two positive choices. "You can use the big potty or the little potty. Which do you choose?" "You can use the upstairs potty or the downstairs potty. What's better for you?" "You can go to the potty by yourself or I can go with you. Which feels most comfortable?"

With all of these examples, either option is acceptable. There's no "wrong" choice like there was in the "big kid" or "baby" example. The phrase "which do you choose" encourages the child to pick one choice or the other without getting sidetracked. This way of framing choices is incredibly useful outside of potty scenarios as well!

Choices: Offering two positive choices gives children a way to comply while still maintaining a degree of autonomy and control over a situation. Choices are an essential strategy for the younger years when children are developmentally inclined to exert control over their world—sometimes rather dramatically!

To offer two positive choices, think of two acceptable outcomes and offer them like this: "You may ___ or ___, which is better for you?" Be certain both are viable options ("You can walk to the car or skip to the car") rather than a desirable option and an undesirable one or a threat ("Go to the car or you're going to miss dinner with Mimi"). A positive choice paired with a negative choice or threat is an attempt at manipulation rather than a true choice, and is likely to be met with resistance. "The Skill of Choices helps children choose compliance and facilitates their ability to focus on the task at hand," Dr. Becky Bailey, *Conscious Discipline: Building Resilient Classrooms.*

In addition to offering clear, positive choices, I can't emphasize enough how important it is to avoid shaming or blaming children when we speak with them about the potty. Questions like "Why did you pee in your pants?" and "Look, Leo uses the potty, why don't you?" are unanswerable and carry an underlying negative intent. These questions are unanswerable because your child doesn't have the conscious awareness or developmental ability to say, *"Well,*

Mom, I peed in my pants because I still have some reluctance about using the potty. Part of me wants to use the potty and part of me isn't sure. And, sometimes I get confused by my body signals. I don't know if there's going to be a little toot or if I actually have to poop. Sometimes, I think I can hold my pee inside and then I'm really surprised when it all gushes out! I'm still learning."

Additionally, asking "why" questions to young children asks them to make up a story. Feeling the unspoken negative intent of these types of questions, the story they make up will often be that they're doing something wrong or bad. At their developmental age, young children can't differentiate between the actions being bad and them being bad. So, they tend to internalize these questions/stories as "I am bad" or "I am wrong." Clearly, this does nothing to help the pottying process or the development of the child's healthy sense of self.

Here's a general guideline: Don't ask a young child a "why" question unless you are talking about science like, "Why does the sky get so dark at night?" or "Why do you think the grass is green instead of brown?" Let your children ask you the "why" questions and answer them! But remove "why" from behavior-based conversations with your child, including pottying. For young children, behavioral "why" questions often imply they've done something wrong and create a negative self-perception rather than promote their self-awareness (and you're not going to get the response you want anyway)!

Authentic Praise

You would think that constant reminders and conversation about the potty would be helpful to a child by keeping the potty foremost in their minds. That's not the case. Constant attention to the potty and conversations about the potty puts pressure on your child, and with pressure comes resistance – just what we want to avoid.

So be cool. You want to convey "it's not a huge deal" both with your conversation and tone. It's important, sure. But this potty thing? It's not the end of the world if it doesn't happen right away. We've got all the time we need. You'll also want to maintain your cool when your child does poop and pee in the potty. Most parents assume success calls for an all-out party, complete with heavy doses of fanfare and lots of unbridled enthusiasm. Again, not necessarily helpful. An over-the-top response can overwhelm your child. They can easily feel pressured, *"This matters so much to Mom and Dad!"* It can promote a deer-in-the-headlights effect, causing them to freeze up, halting their efforts. Or even worse, experience performance anxiety. Plus, kids are great at reading nonverbal signals. If you're faking or exaggerating, the mismatch between what they subconsciously feel and what they consciously hear spells trouble for the potty mastery process.

Instead, be authentic in your praise. Authentic praise is clearly focused on what the child has accomplished, not how you feel about it. It feels real, not theatric. Instead of piling on praise and over-the-top antics, use the skill of noticing to reflect back to your child what they accomplished. Try saying, "You did it! You took care of your body by putting your pee (or poop) in the potty!" Avoid judgment-based statements like, "I like
how you kept your underwear clean!" and "I'm proud of you for using the potty." Those statements describe how you feel about their accomplishment instead of focusing on the accomplishment itself. It's a small difference, but an important one. The occasional "good job" isn't going to sink any ships, just realize there are more meaningful ways to praise your child's efforts. The top three phrases for authentic praise are:

> Way to go!
> You did it!
> You __(describe the action without judgment)__!

If Your Child Feels Like Giving Up

Who doesn't love novelty? The new potty, the new books, the new underwear – they're pretty exciting... at first. Sometimes, especially once the novelty wears off, children began feeling less enthusiastic about the work that goes into potty mastery. After all, diapers are easy and familiar, and you don't have to stop playing when you have to go. Maybe this whole potty thing just isn't worth it.

This ambivalence in and of itself isn't a problem. It's normal and healthy. It becomes a problem when there are prolonged signs of stress with little or no progress. It is also a problem when the *adult's* enthusiasm also begins to wane. "Maybe they're too young," you might think. "We should have waited." Or "This was just a try-out. I wasn't actually sure they were ready." The key is to be able to differentiate between the two. Is your child truly the one who isn't ready, or are you getting caught up in what equates to normal levels of ambivalence or frustration?

Learning new skills is stressful, for both children and adults. In order to grow and expand, we must temporarily leave our comfort zone. This can feel both difficult and uncomfortable! With time and practice, we become more proficient, gain confidence and internalize the skill. As our competence grows, our stress levels decline.

Learning new skills can feel stressful, until these skills are practiced over and over again and they no longer feel new! This is true for both children and adults. However, sometimes it's hard for parents to recognize why toileting feels big for children when it's automatic for us. That's why I created this potty equation:

Early-stage potty learning: Effort > Ease
Mid-stage potty learning: Effort = Ease
Later-stage potty mastery: Effort < Ease

I call this growth experience the "rubber-band" analogy: learning a new skill is like stretching a rubber band. The stretch is the stress — it represents moving away from the familiar into the unfamiliar until the new skill is mastered.

The stretch of the rubber band — this stress — can feel different, tight and uneasy, but it's not going to hurt the child. In fact, this healthy stretch is necessary for growth to occur.

Too much stretch, however, will break the rubber band, just as too much stress can become unhealthy.

Keep in mind that a big change in your parent-child dynamic can be a foreshadowing that your child will resist using the toilet. If you find that most of your interactions with your child are now toilet centric, i.e., almost exclusively centered around your child's toilet usage, the shift in your relationship will feel significant to your child. But they won't have the words to express this. Their experience of sharing time and space with you – as a team – and then having it replaced by your hyper vigilance over their toileting, won't feel good, comfortable or safe. From your child's perspective, they've lost the ease and comfort of peeing and pooping wherever and whenever they want, and they've also lost the unburdened attention they previously experienced from you prior to beginning their potty journey.

A potty reset is in order when a child's toilet learning starts to disrupt aspects of daily living, including eating, sleeping, bath time, and playtime. This isn't an exact science, but it does require you to check-in with yourself. You're the expert on your child – you know when something feels off a little, and you know when something feels off a lot! You'll need to discern if your child's behavioral changes are temporary and part of their new adjustment. Or, if their actions indicate that the potty, and all its associated expectations, are just too overwhelming, for right now.

If you feel like your child is experiencing unhealthy stress levels surrounding potty mastery, there's a solution: Take a "reset." Have a calm, empathetic conversation with your child in which you let them know that they will be going back to diapers for a while. Use noticing and authentic praise to highlight all the ways they worked hard at potty mastery, and let them know they will be taking a break from all their hard work. Your child may feel relieved or disappointed or both relieved and disappointed. Validate those feelings and reaffirm that they will have many opportunities to continue their Body Boss journey in the future but right now, they're taking a break. Then take a complete break from the potty talk, the potty books and everything else potty related. Nonchalantly bring back the diapers and diaper cream like it's no big deal— Because potty mastery is no big deal when viewed from the greater framework of your child's mental health.

Do a complete, judgment-free reset by taking potty learning off the agenda and carving out extra connection time to help restore your child's well-being. You can start the process again in a month... or two... or six. A reset is not a failure, it is a healthy life choice. Hold that intent firmly, and you leave the door wide open for the next effort to end in success. Rest-assured, they can do this!

7
Putting It All Together

Remember the first time you sat behind the wheel of a car? Maybe you were nervous. Maybe some aspects felt natural while others felt awkward. You probably didn't nail parallel parking the first time you attempted it. But someone sat in the passenger seat beside you, encouraging and guiding you with every passing mile.

That's your child in the driver's seat, learning the potty. That's you in the passenger seat, providing guidance. They need your calm, confident energy. They want to know, "Can I do this?" Your verbal and non-verbal behavior will communicate, "Yes you can, and I'm here to help." And your child will learn to use the potty whether or not you do a single thing I've described in this book!

You can't control how quickly your child will master the potty, but you can control how you respond to their learning. Staying optimistic and providing encouragement will help both you and your child. Remember, you are your child's pit crew. When your child feels your trust in their ability to do this job, they'll draw confidence from that trust. When they see you focusing on their efforts and their progress, they'll become more comfortable reaching for that next new skill. Your child's got this... and so do you!

You want to be the best pit crew possible for your child. So, remember the three C's of potty mastery: composure, confidence and consistency. Let's go over them, one at a time.

Composure

For your child to master the potty, your composure as a parent is an absolute must. Your child cannot learn to take comfort from you if you're distressed. Your energy is more important than your words. Bring the best of yourself to this developmental learning. Deep breathing is a must. Before entering a potentially frustrating situation, some parents find it helpful to picture a love-filled  moment. Take three deep breaths, muster a mental image of that precious moment, and focus on that feeling rather than on the large puddle in front of you.

Confidence

Your confidence in your child is as important as your composure. For your child to believe they can achieve potty mastery, you must believe they can do it. Your child might feel hesitant at times, and that's normal. They'll be looking to you for the next cue, which is why you must see your child as 100 percent successful before they achieve success. You will radiate that confidence and they'll find comfort in it.

The potty tools we discussed in this book can also enhance your confidence and support your child's success.

Visual Routines: Visual routine cards can serve as an invaluable resource. Young children benefit from visual representations because they think in pictures instead of words. Displaying the three potty sequences as visual routines can reduce your need to over instruct your child by making the potty process both clear and actionable.

Noticing: Noticing encourages reflection and self-awareness. When we notice behavior without judgment, we invite children to reflect on their actions and intentions. Instead of adults labeling the behavior as good or bad, everyone remains focused on the desired goal—the potty!

Encouragement: Encouragement boosts children's confidence in their toileting skills. By providing consistent support, we help children believe in themselves and their ability to master this new skill. This confidence empowers them to persist, learn from their experiences and ultimately achieve success.

Consistency

Be consistent in your pit crew job. Children are malleable and able to flex, but they don't understand ambiguity. Consistency creates predictability and helps children feel safe. When children feel safe, the brain is able to learn. When children feel unsafe, the brain is too preoccupied with seeking safety to focus on learning. Neuroscience indicates that the optimal learning environment is low threat and high challenge. Consistency is essential for "low threat," while potty mastery itself presents the "high challenge." For children to meet the challenge of potty mastery (or any other mastery), you must provide a physically and emotionally safe place for them to learn. Consistent energy, language and routines cultivates this sense of personal safety.

Avoid alternating between diapers and underwear during the potty learning process, except when sleeping. Alternating disrupts consistency and can disrupt children's understanding of this new concept. When children wear underpants consistently, they begin to associate this new garment with using the potty, promoting a clear cause and effect understanding.

Additionally, check-in with your potty energy and make sure it's clear, and not wishy-washy. If it's wishy-washy, you're apt to give mixed signals to your child, which can lead to confusion and derail their progress. Children take comfort in adult leadership that is supportive, reliable and encouraging. This will give them the confidence to move forward, even in the face of their own uncertainty.

A Final Note

Potty mastery is the first of many, many mastery milestones you and your child will move through together. You'll learn how to help your child. You'll learn how to help yourself. You're already building a strong, loving, trusting relationship with your child, and you're doing a great job! Just keep going.

Understanding the physical, cognitive and emotional skills associated with potty mastery will prepare you to champion your child's efforts. The methods outlined in this book are intended to help you reframe your role from potty patroller to potty partner; to help you think outside the box... of diapers.

It's time to flush away the shame, humiliation, unworthiness, stress and rigid practices that have long been associated with children's toileting. Potty mastery is not a set of strategies or a rote to-do list; it's a process that requires flexibility, heartfelt confidence and patience from all involved. And parenting is not a set of best practices; it's a relationship. This book reminds you to tap into your greatest resource — your relationship with your child!

As you and your child embark on this new learning adventure together, remember that potty mastery is just one skill among many your child will develop within the context of your relationship. When you cultivate and maintain a healthy relationship built on trust, empathy, respect and compassion, your child will be positioned to experience success. You've read, you've learned, you've prepped... you are ready to support your child's unique potty mastery process! I'll be holding a place of quiet confidence for you and your child as you navigate this important time together.

Wishing you well,
Joan

Chapter Guide

Chapter 1: Letting Go

- Potty mastery is a skill of daily living that supports children's autonomy, independence, body ownership and healthy maturity.

- You are not in control of your child's toilet learning, your child is! You are your child's pit crew, support system and quintessential encourager.

- Your natural attunement to your child will guide and inform your child's potty learning.

- Words matter! Shift your thinking from "potty-training" to "potty-mastery."

- Training: Something we do to another person with the goal of achieving a specific outcome.

  - Habit Training: Continually instructing a child to use the toilet, hoping that with enough repetition the child will learn to pee and poop in the potty.

- Mastery: The process of acquiring a new skill that develops over time.

  - Spontaneous Recognition: Self-mastery in action. A child's innate ability to attune to their body, recognize the need to urinate and defecate, and then use the potty.

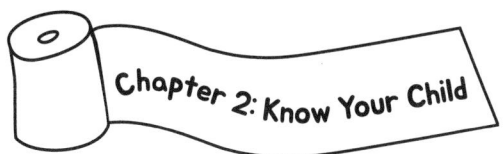

- Consider your child's temperament when supporting their potty learning.

  - Easy temperament: Move forward with gusto!
  - Slow to warm-up temperament: Move slower and avoid overwhelming your child.
  - Strong temperament: Put the power in your child's hands!

- Incentives such as candy, toys, stickers, etc. are not needed for potty learning.

  - An occasional celebratory treat can be helpful for a child who is ambivalent, stalled out, etc.
  - Explore non-tangible treats like dance parties, rituals, and fun activities, instead of food, stickers and toys.
  - Avoid using rewards as a motivator: ~~"If you pee on the potty, you get a sticker."~~ Instead, use celebrations. "You've been working so hard to master the potty, let's celebrate with a trip to the park!"

- Always use your words to illuminate your child's effort, growth and mastery, which will contribute to your child's positive self-esteem.

  - "You're doing it! Using the potty is important work and you're taking good care of your body!"

- Children read their parents' energy and intuitively know that potty mastery feels big.

- Remember to celebrate your child's small, incremental steps towards potty success, just like you did with their earlier milestones of rolling over, sitting-up, crawling, walking, talking, etc.

🧻 The two primary tasks of potty mastery are:

- *Listen* to your body (recognize the need to pee and poop).

- *Take care* of your body (put pee and poop in the potty).

🧻 Before potty learning formally commences, remind your child that they already *listen* to and *take care* of their body.

- Remind them how well they listen to their body when they ask for something to eat or drink.

- Remind them how well they take care of their body when they eat healthy food, wear clean clothes, wash their hands, bathe, clean their scrapes and cuts, etc.

- Once potty learning begins, toileting will become one additional area for them to apply the skills of listening to and taking care of their body.

🧻 Potty mastery includes two parts: The skills of potty mastery and the will of potty mastery.

- Potty mastery **skills** include the integration of the following:

  - Intellectual understanding that pee and poop belong in the potty.

  - Physiological awareness of the need to pee and poop.

  - Time management skills demonstrated in the ability to get to the toilet before having an accident.

- Potty mastery **will** involves:
  - The absence of power struggles.
  - Sustained healthy adult-child attachment.
  - Unconditional regard so a child feels worthy and valued regardless of their success using the potty.

Potty mastery, like dressing, is self-care in action and a sign of your child's growing independence.

Chapter 4: Readiness Signals

Child readiness:

- The child has moved beyond motor-driven play and makes connections and associations with play props. This indicates the child is capable of making the connection that pee and poop belong in the potty.
- The child communicates the need to use the potty verbally or non-verbally.
- The child demonstrates autonomy and self-care by participating in dressing and undressing.

Adult readiness:

- The adult believes the child has the ability to learn new potty skills (this does not mean the child already possess these skills).
- The adult understands that potty mastery is a process, not an event. Time and patience are necessary for this learning to take place. Rushing the process can add stress and derail or lengthen

the amount of time needed for a child to learn potty skills.

- The adult understands that accidents are a necessary and important part of the mastery process.

- Every accident creates a learning opportunity by contrasting the difference between wet/dry and dirty/clean.

- When an adult's efforts are directed at avoiding accidents, the adult acts like a surrogate diaper.

- The adult understands they must manage their own strong emotions connected to their child's potty progress.

Chapter 5: Preparations

Language:

- Script to lose: Don't tell your child they are big and therefore they get to wear big kid underpants.

  - The developmental struggle of a 2-year-old is vacillating between "I want to be a baby!" and "I want to be a big kid!"

- Script to use: Tell your child they will soon have a big and important job; they will be in charge of their body.

  - Children like jobs because all of the important adults in their lives have jobs and they're eager to be a part of the adult world.

- Give their job the title "Body Boss." This identity will help children feel empowered and in control. Then give their Body Boss job a description:
  - Part 1: They listen to their body so they can recognize when they need to pee and poop.
  - Part 2: They take care of their body by putting their pee and poop in the potty.
- Put the Body Boss job into action:
  - "Soon you'll have a new job! It's called being a Body Boss. You get to listen to your body so you recognize when you need to pee and poop. Then you take care of your body by putting your pee and poop in the potty. Being a Body Boss is so awesome and the only person who can do this is you!"
- At the onset of potty mastery, many children will continue to need diapers when they are sleeping, both during naptime and bedtime.
  - Remind your child that when they are asleep, they're off their job and that's why they'll continue to wear diapers (but not for long)!
- When to start:
  - Begin potty learning during a relatively stress-free time for you and your child. Avoid doing it during major transitions such as the start or end of a school program, sickness, new baby, move, out-of-town company or a vacation.
  - Launch the process at home, not at school.
- Things to do:
  - Provide books and play props that support potty

learning. Avoid putting potty props out before you intend to use them.

- Novelty provokes curiosity. If the potty props are available before potty learning commences, you've lost the sweet spot of engaging their curiosity once you begin the process.

- If possible, take your child to the store to purchase underpants, a potty chair or a potty insert for the big toilet, and a stepstool so they have the resources they will need for their new job.

- Find a box that your child can decorate. Label it with your child's name and the words "Sleeping Diapers."

- Make the appropriate changes to your child's physical environment to reinforce the idea that toileting occurs in the bathroom. Remove the changing table pad and transfer creams, lotions and wipes into the bathroom.

Chapter 6: Launching

Involve your child in the transition from diapers to toileting by creating a connecting ritual you and your child can enjoy together, like reading the *Diaper Doggie* book.

- Diaper Doggie visits children at night to replace their diapers with a new pair of underpants so they can begin their Body Boss job!

- To learn more about Diaper Doggie and to purchase the book go to: www.parentstride.com

- Build body awareness through noticing instead of relying on questions. "Your body is squirming like this..." Demonstrate. "Check in with your body. What do you think it's trying to tell you?"

- Celebrate, but avoid over-the-top fanfare when your child successfully uses the potty. Some children can become easily overwhelmed and feel pressured by it. Instead, opt for authentic praise ("Way to go! You used the potty.") Your goal is to help your child become more self-aware by recognizing their accomplishment.

- When it's truly important for your child to use the potty, like before a car trip, say: "It's time to use the potty," or "It's important to use the potty." Avoid micromanaging your child's toileting by constantly reminding them to use the potty.

- When your child has an accident, simply state the facts, "I see your pants are wet/dirty" rather than asking why they had an accident. Also focus your attention on progress and successes. Children are already aware of their oops; pivoting your attention toward something they *did* accomplish shines a light on their effort. Maybe they didn't quite make it to the toilet, but "You recognized your need to potty and went straight to the bathroom!" This is particularly important when your child is making slow progress.

- Avoid weighted choices in which one choice is good and the other choice is not: *"You can act grown-up and use the potty or act like a baby and have accidents."* Instead, offer two positive choices and conclude with the words: "Which do you choose?" For example: "You can use the upstairs potty or the downstairs potty, which do you choose?"

The Rubber Band Analogy Learning:

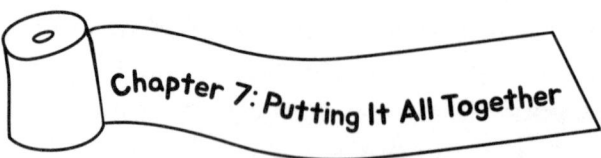

- New skills like mastering the potty can feel stressful. It is analogous to stretching a rubber band.

  - The stress that creates the "stretch" can feel unpleasant but reflects that learning is in motion.

  - If the stress is too overwhelming, the rubber band will "snap".

  - If potty learning begins to erode the child's well-being, a potty reset may be necessary.

Chapter 7: Putting It All Together

- You cannot control how quickly your child will gain potty mastery, but you can control how you respond to their learning.

- The power of your positive thinking combined with large doses of encouragement will go a long way toward success.

The Three C's of Potty Support:

- Composure: Adult composure is a must. A child cannot learn from or take comfort from a distressed adult.

- Confidence: Believe in your child's innate ability to master the potty. Your child will look to you for this reassurance.

- Consistency: Maintain consistent expectation and energy around potty learning. Consistency creates predictability; predictability enhances feelings of safety which optimize the brain for learning.

You've got this! Potty mastery is just one of many opportunities for you to support your child's success!

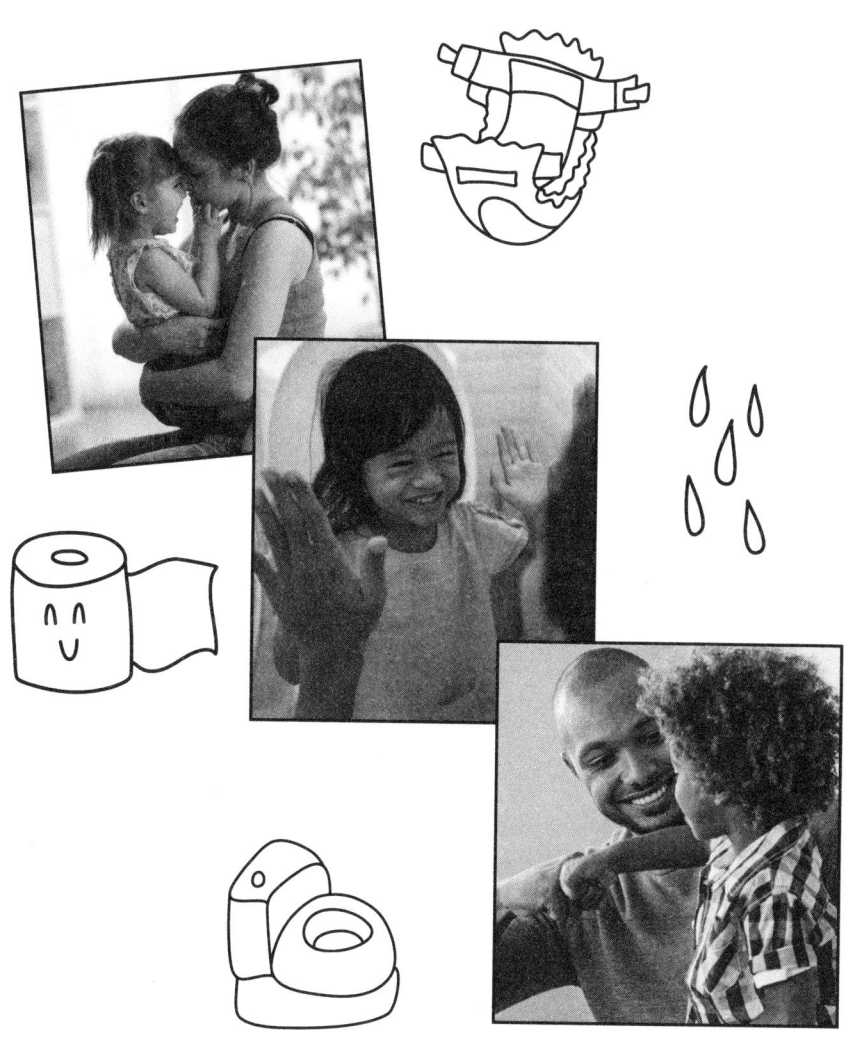